Talent Sourced Volume 2

Modern Search Strategies for <u>Sourcing Talent Online</u>

By: Jonathan Kidder

Legal Disclaimer

The author of the book did not receive any compensation from the companies mentioned in the book for endorsing their tools or websites. He offers his own personal advice on each software tool without any financial incentives. The author assumes no responsibility for any potential harm or legal issues that may arise from using these tools or websites.

It is advisable to seek legal counsel before utilizing any of the recommended tools. Additionally, please conduct research on your country's privacy laws or GDPR regulations before implementing any Software Tools, Boolean strings, or other another suggested ideas from this book.

Table of Contents

About Jonathan Kidder

Jonathan Kidder, known as the "WizardSourcer," is a distinguished technical talent sourcing recruiter, staffing authority, and corporate educator who lends his expertise to organizations of all scales in their pursuit of top-tier talent.

With a wizardly command over the realms of social networking, Boolean strings, search aggregators, deep web exploration, scrapers, and an array of advanced technology tools and techniques, Jonathan has consistently delivered exceptional results.

In 2015, he founded the renowned recruiting blog, WizardSourcer, which has since established itself as a premier source of knowledge for recruiters in the online sphere.

His mission is clear-cut: to empower recruiters and talent sourcers with the latest recruiting tools.

Backed by nearly a decade of experience in full-cycle recruiting and sourcing, Jonathan has contributed his skills to prominent companies like Amazon, Vista Outdoor, CA Technologies, American Express, and many others.

Throughout his career as a sourcing leader, he has remained committed to ongoing education, ensuring he stays at the forefront of sourcing trends and assists clients across diverse industries in optimizing the use of cutting-edge recruiting tools, spanning from browser extensions to AI automation.

Jonathan embarked on his sourcing journey after earning a bachelor's degree in business from Bethel University in Saint Paul, Minnesota, with a role at Allegis Global Solutions, one of the world's largest RPO staffing firms.

It was during his tenure at Allegis that Jonathan recognized the immense potential of social media as a recruiting tool. This revelation inspired him to develop and introduce a proprietary employer branding EVP and recruitment marketing strategy that could be applied to any client's recruitment efforts, attracting the most exceptional talent on a global scale.

A highly sought-after speaker and mentor, Jonathan has conducted training sessions for teams across the world, sharing best practices in sourcing and recruiting top talent. Emerging as a leading authority on recruiting in the 21st century, he regularly contributes his insights to his own top-ranked blog on WizardSourcer, as well as serving as a contributing writer for SourceCon.com and Recruitingblogs.com.

SourceCon 2023- Minneapolis

<u>"Talent Sourced - Volume 2"</u> is an all-encompassing guide that teaches you how to master the entire talent sourcing process within the context of modern talent acquisition.

Whether you're a newcomer or a seasoned Talent Sourcer or Recruiter eager to acquire essential search techniques, this book is specifically crafted to cater to your needs.

Introduction

Talent Sourcing encompasses an entire process within the realm of recruiting. It involves the comprehensive actions of searching for, assessing, selecting, and evaluating potential candidates. This is a specialized skill set that demands a significant upfront investment in understanding its intricacies. Within the pages of this book, you will gain a deep understanding of Talent Sourcing concepts and how to ascend to the level of a masterful search sleuth.

Beyond the rudimentary act of online searching lies the need for expertise in discerning the technical skills and soft skills required to fulfill a job requisition. You must precisely identify the criteria you are seeking and meticulously screen potential candidates based on these fundamental requirements. This book offers a broad perspective on the entire spectrum of talent sourcing, covering everything from online searches and cross-referencing profiles to discovering online communities, securing referrals, and executing pre-screening responsibilities.

To effectively fill a job requisition, it is imperative to actively locate and source candidates within your specific market. Mastering search techniques, understanding what to search for, and adeptly engaging and communicating with candidates are essential skills that you will develop through this comprehensive guide.

This book is meticulously designed as a comprehensive guide to mastering every dimension of Talent Sourcing, tracing its evolution across time. The journey of Talent Sourcing has transformed from the era of flipping through phone books to exploring blogs, chatrooms, forums, diverse web pages in the early days of the internet, and now, it encompasses the sophisticated realm of candidate ranking aided by AI.

In the present, Talent Sourcing revolves around exploring the web of social media communication channels. Virtually every candidate leaves an online trail of information about themselves. While these channels may sometimes pertain to their profession, more often than not, they do not. This book will show you how to leverage this information to cross-reference multiple channels and gain a thorough understanding of a candidate's professional background and experience.

The wealth of online information about a candidate's background can be likened to a modern-day public resume. A candidate might have a LinkedIn profile, share their portfolio on Twitter (X), and maintain a blog on Medium. There are abundant avenues available to connect with potential candidates, and this book will guide you in finding and engaging with these prospects appropriately.

The advent of AI-powered search tools has streamlined the task of centralizing a candidate's comprehensive profile and automating personalized outreach. This embodies the modern approach to talent sourcing in today's digital era, and I aim to provide an in-depth exploration of these advancements in the forthcoming chapters of this book.

This book is intended for the following audiences:

• Newcomers to the field of Talent Sourcing and Recruiting.

• Experienced or self-taught Talent Sourcers and Recruiters seeking a foundational understanding of talent sourcing methods.

• Recruiting Managers interested in optimizing or establishing a new talent sourcing function within their organizations.

This book comprehensively explores the talent sourcing process, offering insights into crafting a highly effective talent sourcing strategy that can ultimately enhance your time-to-fill hiring metrics.

Given the recent integration of AI into Talent Sourcing, I found it imperative to author a second volume in my Talent Sourced book series.

Having an advanced talent sourcing strategy is crucial for several reasons:

Access to Top Talent: Advanced sourcing strategies allow organizations to tap into a broader pool of top talent, including passive candidates who may not be actively seeking new opportunities.

Competitive Advantage: In today's competitive job market, having a well-defined sourcing strategy sets you apart from competitors and helps you secure top talent before they're snatched up by other companies.

Diverse Candidates: Advanced sourcing techniques enable organizations to proactively seek diverse candidates, fostering inclusivity and improving the overall quality of the talent pool.

Reduced Time-to-Fill: Effective sourcing strategies streamline the recruitment process, reducing the time it takes to find, engage, and hire qualified candidates.

Cost Savings: By reducing the time and resources spent on recruitment, advanced sourcing can lead to cost savings in the long run.

Improved Quality of Hire: Advanced strategies allow for more precise candidate targeting, resulting in a higher likelihood of hiring individuals who are an excellent fit for the organization.

Adaptation to Market Changes: The job market is constantly evolving. Advanced sourcing strategies enable organizations to adapt quickly to changes in candidate behavior and market dynamics.

Chapter 1: How has Talent Sourcing Changed?

In the ever-evolving landscape of talent acquisition, the introduction of Generative Artificial Intelligence (AI) has marked a significant turning point. This game-changing technology has revolutionized the way recruiters discover, engage, and ultimately hire top talent. In this chapter, we'll delve into how talent sourcing has undergone a profound transformation with the launch of Generative AI and explore the strategies recruiters should employ to stay ahead of the curve.

The Rise of Generative AI

Generative AI, a subset of artificial intelligence, is designed to generate new content, data, or solutions autonomously, often mimicking human creativity and decision-making processes. In the realm of talent sourcing, Generative AI has brought about several seismic shifts:

Enhanced Candidate Matching

Generative AI can analyze massive datasets to uncover subtle patterns and correlations, allowing for more precise and efficient candidate matching. Recruiters can now identify candidates whose qualifications align closely with job requirements, streamlining the hiring process.

Automated Screening and Engagement

AI-powered chatbots and screening tools have automated the initial stages of candidate interaction.

These tools can engage with candidates, pose qualifying questions, and even conduct basic skills assessments. This automation saves recruiters valuable time, enabling them to focus on more strategic aspects of the recruitment journey.

Personalization at Scale Generative
AI can generate personalized communication and engagement strategies tailored to individual candidate profiles and preferences. This enables recruiters to provide candidates with highly relevant and engaging experiences, enhancing their chances of success.

Data-Driven Decision-Making
AI's ability to analyze historical hiring data offers recruiters valuable insights. By identifying trends and patterns, recruiters can make data-informed decisions regarding job descriptions, sourcing strategies, and interview techniques.

Mitigating Bias in Recruitment
Generative AI focuses on objective criteria, reducing unconscious bias in candidate selection. This is a significant step towards fostering diversity and inclusion in the hiring process.

Adapting to the AI-Driven Future
As recruiters, it's essential to adapt to this AI-driven future. Here's how:

Continuous Learning
Generative AI is continually evolving. Recruiters should invest in ongoing training and development to

stay current with the latest AI advancements in talent sourcing.

Embracing Collaboration
While AI can automate many aspects of talent sourcing, the human touch remains indispensable. Recruiters should view AI as a tool to enhance their capabilities, working in synergy with technology to achieve the best results.

Embrace the Future
Generative AI has reshaped talent sourcing, offering recruiters powerful tools to streamline their efforts and improve candidate quality. By staying informed about AI developments, continuously learning, and fostering a harmonious partnership between human expertise and AI-driven efficiency, recruiters can thrive in this dynamic and evolving recruitment landscape. The future of talent sourcing is here, and it's AI-powered.

Embrace it, adapt, and watch your recruitment efforts reach new heights of success.

Chapter 2: Understanding AI and its Impact

Concerns about the use of AI in talent sourcing are valid and should not be dismissed. However, sourcers have the power to address these concerns by actively monitoring AI systems, balancing automation with human interaction, and prioritizing ethical and fair recruitment practices.

The key is to embrace AI as a valuable tool that enhances the recruitment process, leading to more efficient and effective talent sourcing while upholding the principles of fairness, transparency, and human connection.

Impacts and Benefits:
The introduction of AI in talent sourcing has brought about several transformative benefits:

1. Efficiency: Recruiters can process a larger volume of applications and resumes quickly, focusing their efforts on high-potential candidates.

2. Improved Quality: AI helps identify candidates whose qualifications align closely with job requirements, leading to better matches.

3. Enhanced Candidate Experience: Chatbots and automated communications provide candidates with instant responses and a smoother application process.

4. Data-Driven Decisions: AI offers data insights that aid recruiters in making more informed choices, optimizing the hiring process.

5. Diversity and Inclusion: AI reduces the risk of unconscious bias, promoting diversity in the workforce.

Recruiters are leveraging generative AI in numerous aspects of their workflow to streamline and enhance efficiency. This includes generating interview questions tailored to specific roles, automating calendar scheduling for interviews, crafting compelling job listings and outreach messages, assisting with candidate preparation by suggesting interview strategies, and more.

Chapter 3: Modern Talent Sourcing Tools

Regularly demoing and reviewing the latest talent sourcing tools is essential for recruiters to remain competitive, efficient, and adaptable in the dynamic world of talent acquisition. It enables them to access a wider talent pool, enhance the candidate experience, and make data-driven decisions, ultimately contributing to the success of their organization's recruitment efforts.

Here's a brief glimpse of the advanced recruiting tools at your disposal for talent sourcing. For a comprehensive overview of over 100+ tools, I recommend purchasing my Second Volume of Top Talent Sourcing Tools, available on Amazon.com.

Findem AI
Findem AI is a talent sourcing tool that uses AI to search across various platforms, including job boards, social networks, and professional databases, to find candidates who match specific job requirements.

Harpa AI

HARPA excels at summarizing and responding to emails on your behalf. It can also rewrite, rephrase, enhance, and correct text, as well as read articles, translate languages, and scan web pages for valuable data.

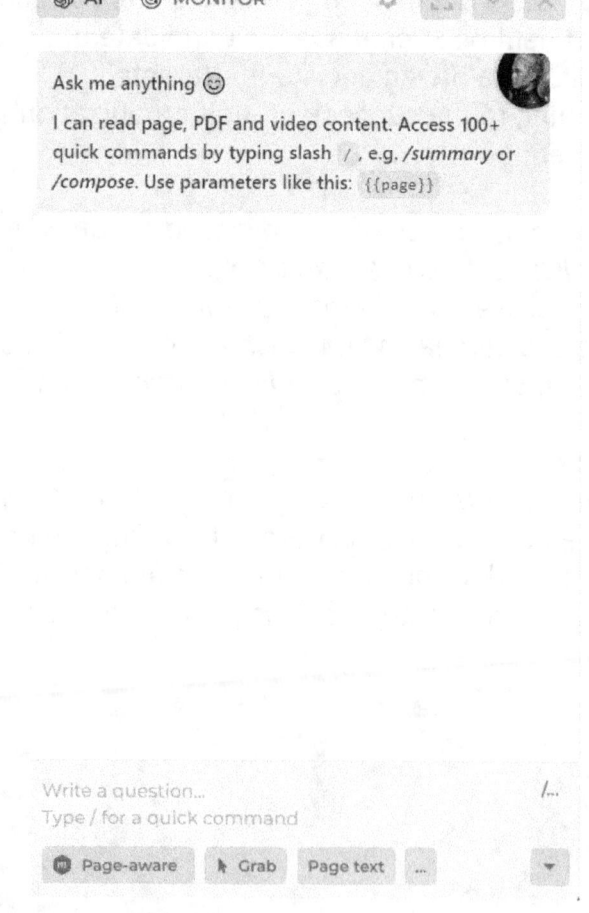

HollyHires AI

HollyHires is an AI-powered recruitment platform that uses machine learning and natural language processing to automate and optimize the candidate selection process. It uses a chatbot-like interface to allow users to ask questions, receive information about job postings, and schedule interviews.

HollyHires claims to be able to save recruiters time and resources by streamlining the recruiting process and reducing bias in the hiring process.

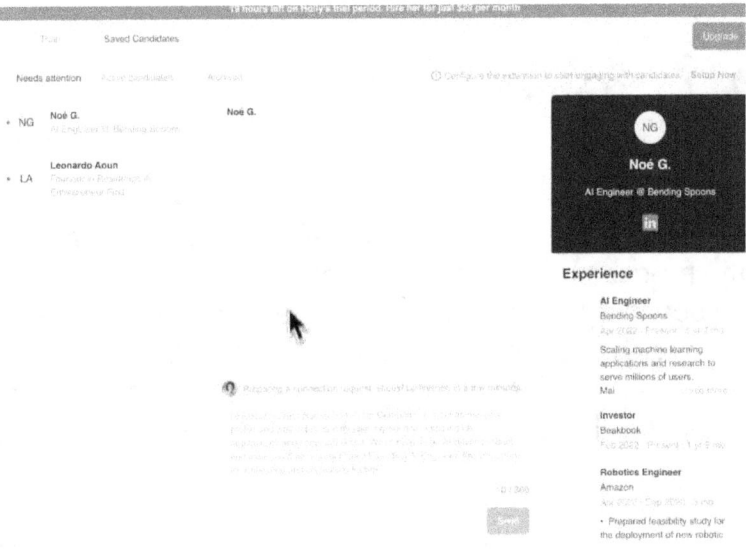

Maxai.me

MaxAI.me is dashboard and chrome extension that supercharges your productivity by amplifying the power of ChatGPT (GPT-4), Claude (Claude 2 100k), Bard, Bing AI, and making it easily accessible at your fingertips! You this tool to create prompts from all the major generative AI tools.

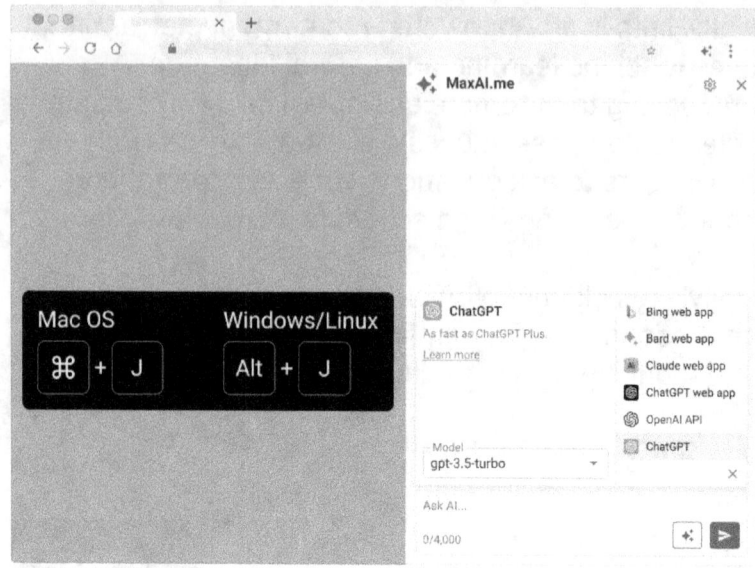

Merlin AI

Merlin AI employs artificial intelligence to automate the process of crafting recruiter outreach messages. By scanning any website page, it enables you to generate a personalized outreach message tailored to that profile. Whether you're on LinkedIn or other websites, this extension tool proves to be incredibly valuable.

Metaview

Metaview leverages AI to assess candidates' soft skills and cultural fit by analyzing video interview responses. Recruiters can gain deeper insights into candidates' personalities and communication styles, facilitating better hiring decisions.

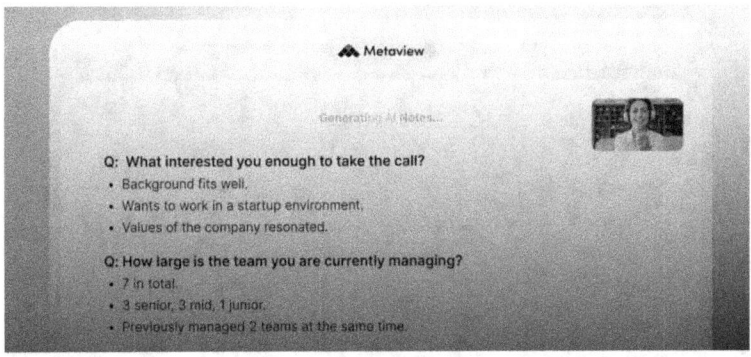

Notion AI

Notion AI leverages AI to automate candidate interviewing, saving recruiters valuable time. It integrates seamlessly with calendar tools and email platforms, making interview coordination more efficient.

PeopleGPT

PeopleGPT offers AI-generated content for candidate outreach, including emails, messages, Recruiters can save time and maintain consistency in their communication with candidates and help automate external talent sourcing efforts.

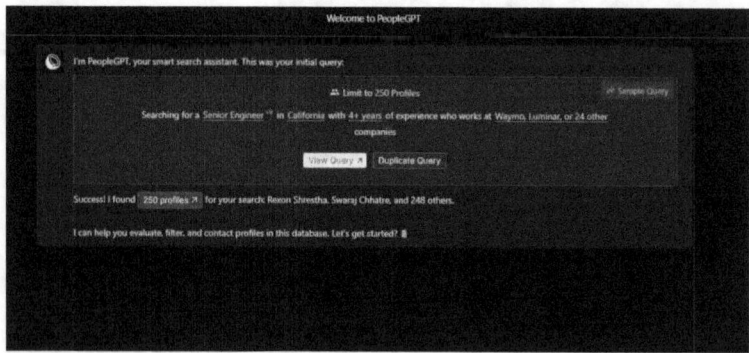

RecruiterGPT

RecruiterGPT, powered by OpenAI's GPT-3, is a versatile AI tool that helps recruiters draft compelling job descriptions, engage candidates through personalized messages, and even conduct preliminary candidate interviews. It streamlines various aspects of the recruitment process, saving time and improving candidate interactions.

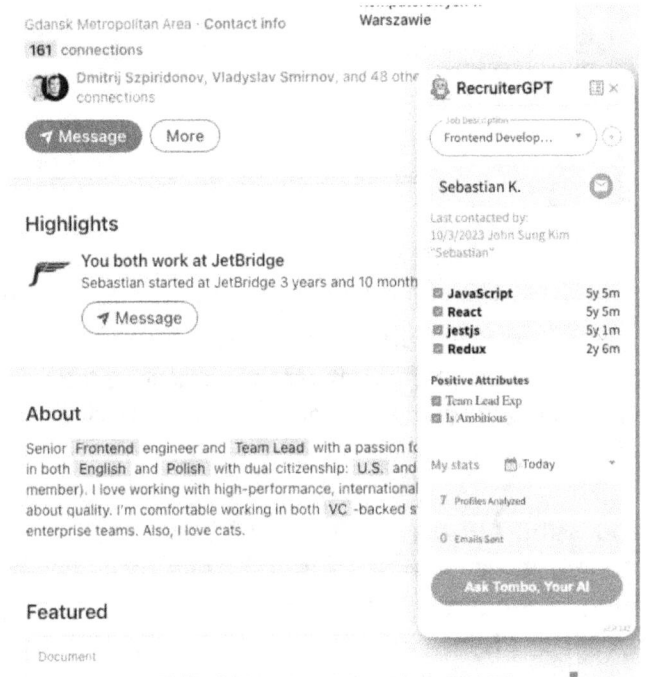

Square Peg

SquarePeg is an end-to-end recruiting automation platform that helps you source, screen, manage, and hire the right talent, faster all the help of AI.

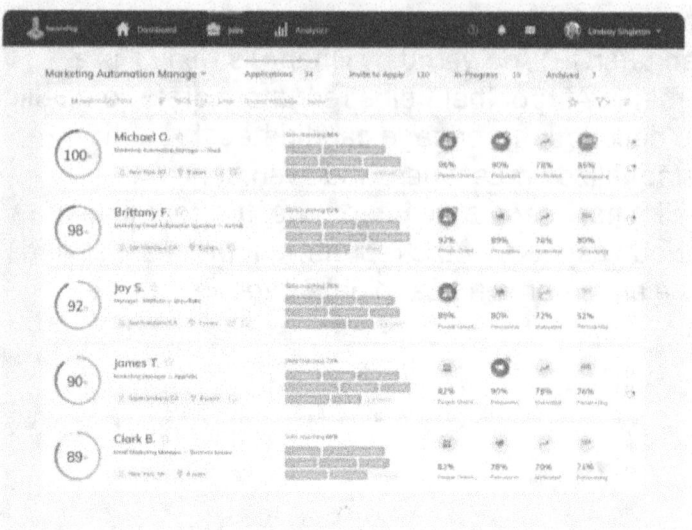

You.com

You.com offers an AI-driven talent search engine that scours the web for candidate information. Recruiters can quickly access publicly available data about potential hires, facilitating more informed sourcing decisions.

Incorporating AI-powered tools into your recruitment arsenal can be a game-changer. These tools offer enhanced efficiency, better candidate insights, and improved candidate experiences. As the recruitment landscape continues to evolve, staying updated with the latest AI innovations can help recruiters gain a competitive edge, attract top talent, and make data-driven hiring decisions.

Chapter 4: Talent Mapping your Data

Recruiters are increasingly inquiring about talent mapping and its role in shaping effective talent sourcing strategies. Leveraging market data is a pivotal aspect of sourcing external leads online. Equally important is integrating this data into your communication with hiring managers.

The process of talent mapping typically involves several steps:

- *Defining the roles and positions that need to be filled, both currently and in the future.*
- *Identifying the key skills and experience required for each role.*
- *Creating a list of potential candidates who possess the required skills and experience, both within the organization and externally.*
- *Gathering and analyzing data on each potential candidate, including their career history, education, skills, and experience.*
- *Creating a detailed profile of each candidate, including their strengths, weaknesses, and potential fit for the role.*
- *Maintaining and updating the talent map on a regular basis to ensure it remains relevant and up-to-date.*

Talent mapping, a strategic process embraced by organizations, empowers recruiters to identify and assess potential candidates within the job market. This proactive approach revolutionizes the way companies understand their talent pool, whether it's within specific industries, functions, or geographic areas.

Key Takeaways on Talent Mapping:

Strategic Planning: Talent mapping serves as a vital component of strategic planning, enabling recruiters to anticipate and plan for current and future talent requirements within their organization.

Proactive Approach: Rather than reacting to immediate job openings, talent mapping allows recruiters to take a proactive stance by identifying potential candidates well in advance.

Market Research: In-depth market research is at the heart of effective talent mapping. It involves gaining a comprehensive understanding of the talent landscape in terms of industries, locations, and even potential competitor talent pools.

Identify Critical Roles: Talent mapping helps in pinpointing critical roles and positions within the organization that require specialized skills or are particularly challenging to fill.

Build Talent Pools: Creating talent pools or pipelines for specific job categories or skill sets is a key outcome of talent mapping. These pools consist of pre-screened candidates ready to be approached when relevant job openings arise.

Data-Driven Decision Making: Talent mapping relies on data and analytics to inform decisions. It includes monitoring talent trends, identifying skills gaps, and staying ahead of market shifts.

LinkedIn Recruiter Insights: LinkedIn Recruiter Insights is an invaluable tool for talent mapping. It offers a wealth of market data and insights, enabling recruiters to revolutionize their talent acquisition strategy.

Leveraging LinkedIn Recruiter Insights

LinkedIn Recruiter Insights provides a treasure trove of market data that can transform the way talent acquisition professionals approach recruitment. Here are some key reasons why it's crucial to harness the power of LinkedIn Recruiter Insights:

Location-Based Talent Search: Utilize LinkedIn's Talent Pool report to conduct talent searches based on location. This can uncover hidden talent gems in unexpected places, making it especially useful for roles like remote software developers.

Data-Backed Expectation Management: LinkedIn Talent Insights offers real-time, accurate data on available talent pools. This data becomes a potent tool for managing hiring managers' and stakeholders' expectations, leading to more realistic and achievable recruitment goals.

Competitive Intelligence for Success: LinkedIn Recruiter Insights provides competitive intelligence that can give you an edge in the talent market. You can analyze growth and attrition rates among companies, guiding your recruitment efforts effectively.

Harnessing BLS.Gov for Talent Mapping
BLS.gov, the Bureau of Labor Statistics website, is another valuable resource for recruiters embarking on talent mapping endeavors. Here's how you can utilize this resource:

Occupational Information: Access detailed information on various occupations, including job descriptions, skills, qualifications, and salary data. This aids in understanding the qualifications and characteristics of sought-after candidates.

Industry Insights: Gain insights into industry trends, growth projections, and regional concentrations. This data helps identify industries with high demand for specific skills or job roles.

Wage Data: Obtain wage data, including national, state, and regional salary information for different occupations. This assists in determining competitive salary ranges when extending job offers.

Labor Market Indicators: Access data on labor force participation rates, unemployment rates, and other labor market indicators. This information paints a clear picture of job market conditions in specific regions.

Occupational Outlook: Explore the Occupational Outlook Handbook for in-depth information on job prospects, growth projections, and occupational outlooks. This data aids in forecasting future talent needs.

Geographic Data: Analyze employment data by geographic area, including metropolitan and non-metropolitan regions. This geographical insight helps target areas with high concentrations of specific skills or industries.

Bringing It All Together: Presenting Talent Mapping Data

Now that you've gathered comprehensive talent mapping data, the next critical step is presenting it effectively to your hiring managers. Here's a step-by-step guide to ensure a successful presentation:

Understand Your Audience: Prioritize understanding your hiring managers' preferences and familiarity with data. Tailor your presentation to meet their specific needs.

Gather and Organize Data: Compile relevant data and structure it logically for easy comprehension. Utilize visual aids like tables, charts, and graphs to enhance clarity.

Define Objectives and Goals: Clearly articulate the objectives and goals of the talent mapping exercise to provide context to your presentation.

Provide Context: Begin with an explanation of why talent mapping is essential, its benefits, and its alignment with the organization's talent strategy.

Highlight Key Findings: Spotlight the most significant findings, such as critical talent gaps, high-potential candidates, and emerging job market trends.

LinkedIn Recruiter Insights (Paid): Incorporate insights from LinkedIn Recruiter Insights, emphasizing the value of data-backed talent decisions.

BLS.Gov (Free Option): Showcase how BLS.Gov data complements your talent mapping efforts, offering a broader perspective on labor market dynamics.

By effectively presenting talent mapping data, you empower your hiring managers with the knowledge they need to make informed decisions, streamline recruitment efforts, and align with the organization's talent strategy. Remember that successful talent mapping is not just about data but also about guiding hiring managers toward actionable steps that will drive your talent acquisition strategy forward.

Chapter 5: Creating a Candidate Persona

Once you have gathered and analyzed Talent Mapping data, the next step is to create candidate personas. A candidate persona is a semi-fictional representation of your ideal candidate for a particular role. It helps you understand the traits, motivations, and aspirations of the candidates you want to attract.

Here's how to create candidate personas using Talent Mapping data:

Segment Your Data: Divide the Talent Mapping data into relevant segments based on factors like job title, location, skills, and experience. This segmentation allows you to create distinct candidate personas for different roles within your organization.

Identify Common Traits: Look for commonalities among the candidates in each segment. What are their career goals? What motivates them? What challenges do they face? By answering these questions, you can start to build a picture of your ideal candidate.

Create Persona Profiles: Develop detailed persona profiles that include information such as age, education, career goals, and pain points. Give your personas names and faces to make them more relatable to your recruitment team.

Tailor Your Messaging: Armed with candidate personas, you can now create targeted messaging that resonates with your ideal candidates. Craft job postings, outreach emails, and marketing materials that speak directly to the motivations and aspirations of your personas.

Benefits of Using Candidate Personas
Creating candidate personas based on Talent Mapping data offers several benefits:

Improved Candidate Quality: By tailoring your recruitment efforts to match the preferences and aspirations of your ideal candidates, you are more likely to attract high-quality talent.

Better Candidate Engagement: Personalized messaging and a deep understanding of candidate personas can lead to higher levels of engagement and interest from potential candidates.

Time and Cost Savings: Targeting the right types of leads reduces the time and resources spent on sifting through unqualified applicants.

In the competitive world of talent acquisition, using Talent Mapping data to create candidate personas is a strategic approach that can significantly enhance your recruitment efforts. By understanding the needs, motivations, and aspirations of your ideal candidates, you can tailor your messaging and outreach to attract the right talent to your organization. Don't underestimate the power of data-driven decision-making when it comes to building a high-performing team that drives your organization's success.

Chapter 6: Conducting the Intake Meeting

One of the crucial steps in the recruitment process is the intake meeting with the hiring manager. This meeting sets the stage for a successful hiring journey by aligning expectations and strategies. In this chapter, we'll explore how to come prepared for an intake meeting with the hiring manager and how to utilize talent mapping and candidate persona information to your advantage.

Part 1: Preparing for the Intake Meeting

1. Research the Role
Before you meet with the hiring manager, it's essential to have a deep understanding of the role you're hiring for. Review the job description, qualifications, and responsibilities. Be ready to ask clarifying questions if anything is unclear.

2. Understand the Organization
Research the company's culture, values, and mission. Familiarize yourself with its industry, competitors, and any recent news or developments. This knowledge will help you align the candidate search with the organization's needs.

3. Prepare a List of Questions
Create a list of thoughtful questions to ask the hiring manager during the meeting. These questions should cover aspects such as the ideal candidate's

qualifications, experience, team dynamics, and long-term goals for the role.

To effectively recruit for a new requisition, recruiters can ask hiring managers a series of questions to gather essential information. Here's a list of questions a recruiter can ask a hiring manager:

Job Role and Responsibilities:
- What is the primary purpose of this role within the organization?
- Can you describe the key responsibilities and tasks associated with this position?
- Are there any specific projects or initiatives this role will be involved in?

Qualifications and Skills:
- What qualifications, certifications, or degrees are required for this role?
- What technical or soft skills are essential for success in this position?
- Are there any industry-specific skills or knowledge that candidates should possess?

Experience and Background:
- What level of experience is ideal for candidates applying for this role?
- Are there any preferred backgrounds or industries from which we should target candidates?
- Is prior experience in a similar role or industry a requirement?

Team and Department:

- How does this role fit into the broader team and department structure?
- What is the reporting structure for this position?
- Can you describe the team dynamics and culture?

Goals and Objectives:
- What are the short-term and long-term goals for the individual in this role?
- How does this role contribute to the department's or company's overall objectives?

Performance Metrics and Expectations:
- What key performance indicators (KPIs) or metrics will be used to evaluate the success of the person in this role?
- What are the performance expectations for the first three, six, and twelve months?

Candidate Profile:
- What does the ideal candidate look like in terms of skills, experience, and personality traits?
- Are there any specific attributes or qualities you are looking for in candidates?

Recruitment Timeline:
- What is the expected timeline for filling this position?
- Are there any critical deadlines or time-sensitive projects related to this role?

Interview Process:

- Can you outline the interview process, including the number of interview rounds and the key stakeholders involved?
- Are there any specific assessments or tests that candidates will be required to complete?

Compensation and Benefits:
- What is the salary range and compensation package for this role?
- Are there any unique benefits or perks associated with this position?

Company Culture and Values:
- Can you describe the company's culture and core values?
- Are there specific cultural attributes that you'd like candidates to align with?

Diversity and Inclusion:
- Are there diversity and inclusion goals for this hiring process?
- How does this role contribute to the company's diversity initiatives?

Onboarding and Training:
- What onboarding and training resources will be available to the new hire?
- Are there specific training programs or certifications required for this role?

Additional Information:
- Is there any other information or context about the role that would be helpful for candidates to know?

- Do you have any specific preferences or criteria for sourcing candidates?

Closing Questions:
- Are there any questions or concerns you have about the recruitment process or the candidates we should address?
- What are the next steps in the recruitment process?

4. Review Candidate Personas
Utilize candidate personas based on talent mapping data to guide your conversation. Knowing the traits, motivations, and preferences of your ideal candidates will help you tailor your discussion and align it with the personas' characteristics.

Part 2: Setting Good Expectations

1. Communicate Realistic Timelines
Discuss the expected timeline for the hiring process, from posting the job to making the final offer. Highlight potential bottlenecks and factors that may affect the schedule, such as multiple interview rounds or candidate availability.

2. Clarify the Hiring Criteria
Work with the hiring manager to define the must-have and nice-to-have qualifications for the role. Clearly communicating these criteria will help streamline the candidate evaluation process and avoid any misunderstandings later on.

3. Discuss Sourcing Strategies

Leverage your talent mapping data to suggest sourcing strategies that align with the personas you've created. Whether it's tapping into specific talent pools, utilizing social media, or reaching out to industry-specific networks, set clear expectations on how you plan to find the ideal candidates.

4. Establish Communication Protocols

Determine how you and the hiring manager will communicate throughout the hiring process. Discuss preferred communication channels, frequency of updates, and who should be involved in decision-making.

Part 3: Using Talent Mapping and Candidate Persona Info

1. Targeted Outreach

Leverage your candidate personas to create compelling job postings and outreach messages that resonate with your ideal candidates. Use the information from talent mapping to identify where these candidates are most likely to be found.

2. Screen Candidates Effectively

When reviewing resumes and conducting interviews, refer back to your candidate personas. Look for candidates who align with the traits and qualifications you've identified, increasing the chances of finding the right fit.

3. Engage Candidates Thoughtfully

During interviews and interactions with candidates, use the insights from your personas to ask relevant questions and address their motivations and concerns. This personalized approach can help build stronger connections.

4. Report Progress and Adjust
Regularly update the hiring manager on your progress, including the number of candidates sourced, interviewed, and their qualifications. If necessary, be prepared to adjust your sourcing and screening strategies based on real-time feedback.

5. Presenting Candidates
Presenting a slate of candidates to a hiring manager is a critical step in the recruitment process. It involves effectively communicating the qualifications, strengths, and potential fit of each candidate. Here's a step-by-step guide on how to present a slate of candidates to the hiring manager:

Compile Candidate Profiles:
Collect detailed information about each candidate, including their resumes, cover letters, interview feedback, assessment results, and any other relevant documents.

Organize the Information:
Create a document or digital presentation that neatly organizes candidate information. You can use a spreadsheet, document, or applicant tracking system (ATS) to keep everything organized.

Prioritize Candidates:
Prioritize the candidates based on their qualifications, skills, and alignment with the job requirements.

Highlight the top candidates who are the best fit for the role.

Include Key Information:
For each candidate, provide key information such as their name, current position, relevant experience, education, and notable achievements.

Summarize Strengths:
Highlight the strengths, skills, and experiences that make each candidate stand out. Be specific about how their qualifications match the job requirements.

Final Round Preparation:
Understanding the business and the role is critical when influencing a debrief because it allows you to make informed decisions and provide relevant insights during the discussion.

Final round debrief discussions:

1. Understanding bias
Bias is your brain using shortcuts to come to a rational decision.

To mitigate the impact of bias during the interviewing process, it is important to establish clear evaluation criteria and to train interviewers on how to recognize and avoid bias. It is also important to have a diverse interview team and to structure the interview process in a way that ensures that candidates are evaluated fairly and objectively.

Bias can play a significant role in the interviewing process, often leading to unfair and discriminatory practices that negatively impact the candidate experience and the quality of the hiring decision. Some ways that bias can manifest during the interviewing process include:

Unconscious bias: This is bias that is not intentional, but rather arises from unconscious attitudes, stereotypes, and assumptions that people hold about certain groups of people. For example, a hiring manager may unconsciously assume that a female candidate is less competent than a male candidate, even if there is no evidence to support this belief.

Confirmation bias: This is the tendency to seek out information that confirms our pre-existing beliefs or opinions, while ignoring information that contradicts them. In an interviewing context, this can lead to interviewers asking questions that only support their initial impressions of the candidate, and ignoring evidence that suggests the candidate is a good fit for the position.

Similarity bias: This is the tendency to favor candidates who are similar to ourselves or who share our background or experiences. For example, a hiring manager who went to the same university as a candidate may be more likely to hire that candidate, even if there are other candidates who are more qualified for the position.

Halo effect: This is the tendency to form an overall positive impression of a candidate based on one positive trait or characteristic, even if other aspects of their performance or experience are not strong. For example, an interviewer may give a candidate a high rating based on their impressive educational credentials, even if their work experience is less impressive.

How to challenge bias:
Challenging bias during the final round interview is an important step to ensure that the hiring decision is fair and objective. Here are some strategies that can be used to challenge bias during the final round interview:

Use structured interview questions: Using structured interview questions that are based on the requirements of the job and the candidate's qualifications can help reduce bias by ensuring that all candidates are evaluated on the same criteria.

Encourage diversity on the interview team: Including interviewers with diverse backgrounds and experiences can help to reduce the impact of bias by bringing different perspectives to the evaluation process.

Provide interviewer training: Providing training to interviewers on how to recognize and avoid bias can help them to be more aware of their own biases and to make more objective evaluations of candidates.

Use data-driven decision-making: Using data and analytics to evaluate candidates can help to reduce bias by providing an objective measure of candidate performance and qualifications.

Challenge assumptions: Encouraging interviewers to challenge their assumptions and preconceptions about candidates can help to reduce bias by ensuring that they are evaluating candidates based on objective criteria rather than subjective beliefs or attitudes.

How can recruiters sway the final round discussions?
Do your homework:
- Know the role/team/org
- Review candidate interview feedback
- Bring tangible data points

Set expectations right away – when the debrief starts:
- Discuss role your and say that you will be giving feedback as well
- Don't be afraid to speak up right away and don't wait to be called on.

Chapter 7: Creating a Process Flow

As a new sourcer, you're responsible for finding and attracting top talent to your organization. To do this effectively, you'll need to create a talent sourcing process tailored to your company's unique needs and goals.

Step 1: Understand Your Company's Needs

Before you can start sourcing candidates, it's crucial to gain a deep understanding of your company's hiring goals and requirements. Schedule meetings with hiring managers and other key stakeholders to:

1. Learn about the specific roles you'll be sourcing for.

2. Understand the qualifications, skills, and experience required for each role.

3. Identify any unique challenges or preferences in the hiring process.

4. Clarify the company's values, culture, and employer brand.

Step 2: Develop a Sourcing Strategy

Once you have a clear understanding of your company's needs, it's time to create a sourcing strategy. This strategy should outline how you'll find and attract qualified candidates. Consider the following:

1. **Sourcing Channels:** Determine which platforms, job boards, social media networks, and professional associations are most effective for reaching your target candidates.

2. **Candidate Personas:** Create candidate personas based on the roles you're sourcing for. These personas will help you tailor your sourcing efforts to the preferences and motivations of your ideal candidates.

3. **Networking:** Build relationships with industry professionals, attend relevant events, and engage in online forums and communities to expand your network.

4. **Employer Branding:** Work with your marketing team to enhance your company's employer brand, making it more appealing to potential candidates.

Step 3: Establish Sourcing Tools and Technology

To streamline your sourcing efforts, you'll need the right tools and technology. Consider investing in:

1. **Applicant Tracking System (ATS):** An ATS helps you manage candidate data, track progress, and collaborate with hiring teams.

2. **Sourcing Software:** Tools like LinkedIn Recruiter, Boolean search platforms, and candidate database tools can help you identify and contact potential candidates.

3. **Data Analytics:** Use data analytics to track the effectiveness of your sourcing strategies and make data-driven decisions.

Step 4: Source and Engage Candidates

With your strategy and tools in place, you can now start actively sourcing candidates. Here's how:

1. **Identify Potential Candidates:** Use your sourcing tools to search for candidates who match your job requirements.

2. **Personalized Outreach:** Craft personalized and compelling outreach messages that highlight the value of your company and the specific job opportunity.

3. **Engagement:** Engage with candidates on social media, respond promptly to inquiries, and provide a positive candidate experience.

4. **Maintain a Pipeline:** Keep a steady pipeline of potential candidates even when there are no

immediate job openings. This ensures you're prepared when positions become available.

Step 5: Evaluate and Optimize

Continuous improvement is key to a successful sourcing process. Regularly evaluate your efforts and make necessary adjustments:

1. **Metrics and Analytics:** Monitor the success of your sourcing activities by tracking metrics like candidate response rates, time-to-fill, and source effectiveness.

2. **Feedback:** Solicit feedback from hiring managers and candidates to understand what's working and where improvements can be made.

3. **Adapt and Evolve:** Be adaptable and open to trying new sourcing strategies and technologies as the recruitment landscape evolves.

Using the data to improve your process:

Once you have collected your recruiting data, it is essential to determine how you will act on it. Here are some examples of common recruiting issues that data can help uncover, along with ways to address them:

Time to hire: If your time-to-hire is consistently higher than industry standards, you may need to identify and address bottlenecks in your recruiting process. You can consider diversifying your sourcing methods, including qualifying questions on your application forms, using software to schedule interviews, and writing effective job offer letters.

Low offer acceptance rates: If you are experiencing a high percentage of job offer rejections, you may need to create more competitive job offers, gauge candidate interest early on, ensure a positive candidate experience, and write job offer letters that accurately reflect the role.

High new hire turnover: If your new hire turnover is too high, you may need to improve communication with candidates about job duties and requirements, create an effective onboarding process, and provide opportunities for meaningful work.

It's important to note that data has its limitations. While it can provide insight into what your team does well and areas that need improvement, it cannot explain why something is happening. Interpreting your findings requires a combination of different types of data and human judgement. Ultimately, what you choose to do with the data is at your discretion.

Step 6: Streamline the Hiring Process

Streamlining the hiring process can be important for attracting and retaining top talent, reducing time to fill, and improving the overall candidate experience. Here are some ways to streamline the hiring process:

Define job requirements: Clearly define the job requirements, including the skills and experience needed for the role. This will help you to focus your search and quickly identify qualified candidates.

Use targeted job postings: Use targeted job postings to reach potential candidates who have the specific skills and experience needed for the role. This can help to reduce the number of unqualified applicants and streamline the screening process.

Use an applicant tracking system (ATS): An ATS can help to automate the recruitment process, including job postings, resume screening, and candidate communication. This can help to reduce manual work and make the process more efficient.

Implement pre-employment testing: Pre-employment testing can help to identify top candidates quickly and objectively. This can help to reduce the time it takes to screen candidates and move them through the hiring process.

Standardize interview questions: Standardizing interview questions can help to ensure that all candidates are asked the same questions, making it easier to compare and evaluate candidates. This can help to streamline the interview process and reduce the time it takes to make hiring decisions.

Use video interviews: Video interviews can help to save time and reduce the need for in-person interviews. This can be particularly useful for initial screenings or for candidates who are located in different geographic regions.

Use reference checks strategically: Use reference checks to gather additional information about the top candidates, but use them strategically to avoid delays in the hiring process.

Chapter 8: Creating a Talent Sourcing Strategy

One of your primary responsibilities is to find and attract top talent. To do this effectively, it's crucial to create a well-thought-out talent sourcing strategy. This strategy will help you identify, engage, and eventually hire the best candidates for your organization.

Step 1: Understand the Job Requirements
Before you dive into sourcing candidates, it's essential to have a crystal-clear understanding of the job requirements. Start by having a detailed conversation with the hiring manager to ensure you're both on the same page. Key points to discuss include:

Job Responsibilities: Clarify the specific duties and responsibilities associated with the role.

Qualifications: Understand the qualifications, skills, and experience required for the position.

Level of Flexibility: Determine whether the hiring manager is open to candidates who may not meet all requirements but have the potential to excel.

Step 2: Create an Ideal Candidate Profile
With a solid understanding of the job requirements, create an ideal candidate profile. This profile outlines the characteristics, skills, and traits that define your perfect hire. Consider factors such as:

Experience: Define the ideal candidate's level of experience in years.

Skills: Identify the key technical and soft skills required for success in the role.

Cultural Fit: Consider how the candidate will fit into the company culture.

This candidate profile will serve as a benchmark when evaluating potential candidates.

Step 3: Start with Former Candidates
Begin your talent search by revisiting candidates who applied for similar positions in the past but were not selected. These silver and bronze medalists, as we like to call them, already expressed interest in your company. Utilize your applicant tracking system (ATS) or candidate relationship management system (CRM) to access their data and build your sourcing pipeline.

Step 4: Build and Maintain Your Sourcing Pipeline
Your sourcing pipeline is a valuable asset. It's a repository of potential candidates, including passive candidates who may not be actively seeking new opportunities. Keep this pipeline active by consistently adding new candidates who align with your candidate personas and company culture.

Remember, candidates who previously applied to your company are more likely to respond to your outreach efforts.

Step 5: Look to the Future

Encourage your sourcers and recruiters to keep an eye on the horizon. Predict future hiring needs based on your company's growth plans and evolving business requirements. By identifying potential talent in advance, you gain a competitive edge and are better prepared for upcoming workforce changes.

Step 6: Expand Your Search
Don't limit your search to basic or common keywords. Use advanced search techniques to uncover hidden gems. Consider using Boolean search operators and exploring alternative job titles that candidates might use for similar roles.

Step 7: Mind Passive Candidates
While passive candidates can be a valuable resource, use your time wisely. Ensure that passive candidates you engage with are genuinely interested in exploring new opportunities. Passive candidates may have outdated profiles on platforms like LinkedIn, so be prepared for this.

Step 8: Track Sourcing and Recruiting Metrics
Implement a data-driven approach by tracking key metrics, such as:

Response Rates: Measure how many outreach attempts it takes to get an initial response from a candidate.

Engagement: Analyze which outreach messages are most effective in garnering responses.

Nurturing Time: Determine how long it takes to nurture a candidate and persuade them to apply.

Time-to-Hire: Track the time from the initial interview of a sourced candidate to their eventual hire. These metrics provide insights into where top talent is hiding and help you optimize your sourcing approach.

Step 9: Build Your Employer Brand
Invest in your employer brand to attract potential talent. Consider what sets your company apart and create an emotional connection with potential candidates. Leverage social media platforms like Instagram to build and showcase your employer brand.

Step 10: Use Social Media and Various Platforms
Leverage social media platforms, job boards, and specialized networks to streamline your sourcing efforts. Tools like LinkedIn, Indeed, Facebook, Twitter, Slack, and Meetup can be invaluable in identifying and engaging with candidates.

Step 11: Think Outside the Box
Explore unconventional sourcing channels where your target candidates congregate online. For instance, Behance is excellent for creatives, while GitHub is a treasure trove for developers. Share your company's unique story and initiatives to capture candidates' attention.

Step 12: Consider Internal Talent

Don't overlook internal talent. Look within your organization for employees who may be suitable for new roles or promotions. This approach is especially effective for succession planning.

Step 13: Employee Referrals

Tap into the power of employee referrals. Encourage your employees to refer qualified candidates and consider implementing an employee referral program. Employee referrals can significantly reduce time-to-hire and improve retention rates.

Step 14: Embrace AI in Sourcing

Harness the capabilities of AI in sourcing to automate and enhance your candidate search. AI can help identify suitable candidates efficiently, reducing time-to-fill and cost-per-hire.

Building a comprehensive talent sourcing strategy after an intake meeting with the hiring manager is a crucial step in finding the right candidates for your organization. By following these steps and staying agile in your approach, you'll be well-equipped to identify, engage, and hire top talent while optimizing your sourcing efforts. Remember, sourcing is a dynamic process that requires continuous improvement and adaptation to the ever-changing talent landscape.

Chapter 9: Talent Sourcing and Searching Online

In today's competitive job market, finding the right candidates for your organization requires more than just posting job listings and waiting for applications to pour in. Successful recruitment demands a proactive approach that leverages advanced techniques to search and source candidates online. In this blog post, we will explore some cutting-edge methods and strategies to help you identify top talent effectively.

1. Boolean Search Magic

Boolean search is a powerful technique that allows recruiters to craft highly specific search queries on search engines, social media platforms, and professional networking sites. By combining keywords with operators like "AND," "OR," and "NOT," you can refine your searches and discover candidates with precision. Mastering Boolean search can unlock a treasure trove of hidden talent.

Example:

- "Software engineer" AND ("Python" OR "Java") NOT "junior" site:linkedin.com

2. Social Media Mining

Social media platforms are rich sources of candidate data. Beyond LinkedIn, platforms like Twitter, Facebook, and Instagram offer valuable insights into a candidate's interests, skills, and professional activities. Tools like Twitter Advanced Search and Facebook Graph Search enable you to uncover potential candidates who might not have a strong presence on traditional job boards.

3. Chrome Extensions and Tools

Chrome extensions can be a sourcer's best friend. Tools like Hunter (for email address discovery), Lusha (for contact information), and Clearbit (for enrichment) can turbocharge your candidate sourcing efforts. These extensions seamlessly integrate into your browser, making it easy to access candidate information with a single click. I recommend reading my "Top Talent Sourcing Tools for Recruiters," book series if you want to learn more.

4. X-Ray (SITE) Searches

X-ray searches involve using search engines to comb through specific sites or domains. For instance, you can use the "site:" operator to search for candidates on a particular website, such as a university's faculty page or a company's employee directory. This method can help you find candidates with specialized skills or backgrounds.

Example:

- site:example.com "data scientist"

5. Advanced LinkedIn Search

LinkedIn is a goldmine for professional networking and candidate sourcing. However, you can take your LinkedIn searches to the next level by using filters and operators. You can filter by location, industry, company size, and more. Additionally, you can employ Boolean operators and wildcards in your searches for greater precision.

6. Talent Communities and Forums

Online communities and forums related to your industry or niche are often teeming with potential candidates. Participate in these communities, engage in discussions, and discreetly identify individuals with the skills and expertise you seek. Websites like GitHub, Stack Overflow, and Reddit can be particularly valuable for tech-related roles.

7. Alumni Networks

Leverage the power of alumni networks from universities and colleges. Many educational institutions maintain online directories or LinkedIn groups for their alumni. These networks can be excellent sources for finding candidates with specific educational backgrounds or degrees.

8. Hackathons and Coding Challenges

Tech-savvy candidates often participate in hackathons, coding challenges, or open-source projects. Websites like GitHub and Kaggle host coding competitions where you can identify individuals who excel in problem-solving and coding. Reach out to participants who match your criteria.

9. Niche Job Boards

While traditional job boards are well-known, niche job boards cater to specific industries or job roles. Consider exploring these specialized platforms to find candidates who are deeply passionate about and experienced in your industry. Examples include Behance for creatives and Dice for tech professionals.

10. Artificial Intelligence and Machine Learning

Embrace the future of recruitment with AI and machine learning tools. These technologies can analyze vast amounts of data to identify potential candidates who match your criteria. AI-driven chatbots and virtual assistants can also streamline candidate engagement and pre-screening processes.

Mastering advanced candidate sourcing techniques online is essential in today's competitive talent landscape. By combining Boolean search, social media mining, Chrome extensions, X-ray searches, and other advanced methods, you can uncover hidden talent pools and identify the perfect candidates for your organization. Stay proactive, adaptable, and tech-savvy to stay ahead in the recruitment game and build a stellar team that propels your organization to success. Happy sourcing!

Chapter 10: Boolean Strings

Sourcing candidates online can be a daunting task, especially in a sea of information overload. Sourcers need to possess the ability to refine their searches and navigate through the vast digital landscape to find the right talent. In this guide, we'll explore advanced techniques and strategies to help sourcers pinpoint specific information quickly and effectively.

Choosing the Right Search Engine

Not all search engines are created equal, and each has its unique features and limitations. Understanding the differences between them is essential for successful candidate sourcing. Here are some insights into the most commonly used search engines:

Google

- Word Order Matters: Google ranks keywords in the order they appear.

- Operators and Modifiers: Google supports various operators like (), "", NOT, -, OR, and more.

- Maximum Keywords: You can use up to 32 keywords in each search.

Bing

- Default AND Searches: Bing performs AND searches by default.

- Capitalized Operators: You must capitalize NOT and OR for them to work correctly.

- Stop Words: Common stop words are ignored unless enclosed in quotation marks.

- Limited Keywords: Bing uses only the first ten terms for search results.

DuckDuckGo

- Multiple Sources: DuckDuckGo gathers results from various sources.

- No Predictable Count: Due to its unique result generation, it doesn't display the number of results.

- Supports Standard Operators: DuckDuckGo uses standard operators similar to Google.

Pro Tip: Consider specialized search engines like Google Scholar for academic articles or WolframAlpha for data and statistics in talent mapping.

Searching on Specific Websites

Directly searching on a website like LinkedIn or Facebook can yield different results compared to a search engine. It's often more efficient to perform a site-specific search for precise results.

Understanding Boolean Operators and Modifiers

Boolean search strings are powerful tools for sourcers, enabling them to refine their searches effectively. Here are some fundamental Boolean operators:

AND

Use the "and" operator to broaden your search by combining multiple keywords. Google no longer requires "AND" in searches; a space between keywords suffices.

Example:

- content writer AND editor

- graphic designer AND photographer

OR

The "OR" operator helps find candidates with alternative skills or roles.

Example:

- content AND writer OR creator OR developer

- customer service AND tech support OR technical support

NOT

The "not" operator excludes specific terms from your search.

Example:

- content AND writer OR editor NOT developer

Additional Modifiers

- Parentheses (): Use parentheses to give priority to certain words.

- Quotes "": Enclose terms in quotes for exact matches.

- Wild Card (*): Use the asterisk as a wildcard for keyword variations.

Using Boolean search strings allows you to create precise queries to find the best candidates.

Let's dive into these advanced Google search operators and discover how they can supercharge your candidate search.

1. site:example.com
This is your entry point into Google's advanced search operators. By using site:example.com, you instruct Google to search within a specific website or domain. It's perfect for narrowing down your candidate hunt to a particular company's website.

2. site:example.com/folder

Take your search one step further with this operator. If you want to explore a specific sub-folder on a website, simply add /folder to the end of the domain, and Google will focus your search within that area.

3. site:sub.example.com
For delving into sub-domains of a website, the site:sub.example.com operator is your go-to choice. It's handy when a company's various departments or divisions have separate sub-domains.

4. site:example.com inurl:www
Adding inurl:www to your search allows you to find URLs within the specified domain that include "www." But here's the twist: by adding a "-" in front of it (e.g., -inurl:www), you can exclude URLs with "www," giving you a different perspective on the website's content.

5. Chain Operators to Get More Done
Recruiting demands precision, and chaining operators allows you to achieve just that. Combine different operators to create specific search queries. For example: site:example.com -inurl:www -inurl:dev -inurl:shop.

6. site:example.com inurl:https
Security matters. Use this operator to find secure (HTTPS) pages on a website. It's essential when you're looking for candidates with expertise in secure web development or other related fields.

7. site:example.com inurl:param
Worried about tracking down pages with specific parameters? The inurl:param operator comes to your

rescue, helping you navigate pagination and other sorting mechanisms on websites.

8. site:example.com -inurl:param
Curious about the total number of pages indexed on a website? Use -inurl:param to exclude URLs with parameters and get a clearer picture of the website's content size.

9. site:example.com text goes here
Combine the site operator with a plain text query to search a website's entire content for specific keywords. Google will try to match all the terms you enter, making it a powerful tool for comprehensive searches.

10. site:example.com "text goes here"
For pinpoint precision, surround your text with quotation marks. This operator ensures an exact match, ideal for tracking down specific details on a website.

11. site:example.com/folder "text goes here"
You can apply the exact match operator to specific website folders as well. Whether you want an exact match or any relevant results, this operator does the job.

12. site:example.com this OR that
When you're unsure of the exact term you're looking for, use "OR" in your query to explore multiple options. It's a useful operator for finding candidates with diverse skillsets or qualifications.

13. site:example.com "top * ways"
The asterisk (*) acts as a wildcard, allowing you to search for unknown text. This operator comes in handy when you're exploring innovative approaches or solutions.

14. site:example.com "top 7..10 ways"
If you have a specific number range in mind for your search, employ the "X...Y" format. Google will return results falling within that range. It's a fantastic way to narrow down your options.

15. site:example.com intitle:"text goes here"
The intitle operator is your ticket to searching for text specifically within <TITLE> tags on a website. It helps you focus on content that holds particular significance.

16. "text goes here" -site:example.com
This operator allows you to find text across the entire web while excluding a specific domain. It's perfect when you're trying to uncover information about a company or candidate outside of their primary website.

17. site:example.com filetype:pdf
If you're on the hunt for documents of a particular file type, the filetype operator is your ally. In this example, you can find all PDFs within a specified domain. Feel free to adapt it for other file formats.

Pro Tip: robot.text (SITE) Searches:

Understanding robots.text on a website:

The robots.txt is a game changer. Also inspecting sitemaps is a great avenue for sourcing. For example, you'll see 2 links from the devops .com site where you can retrieve author profiles. The good news is every author profile has an email address (just hover your mouse to the envelope icon). You can scrape it and then upload it to a data enrichment tool.

https://devops.com/author-sitemap.xml

https://devops.com/author-sitemap2.xml

A thorough understanding of these operators and search techniques will empower users to craft precise and effective Boolean search strings, enhancing their ability to retrieve relevant information online.

People Search Engines

People search directories can provide valuable contact information for candidates. Many of the contact finding extensions buy their data from these types of databases. Instead of using those you can go directly to the source for example Pipl has the largest database of data available online.

Here are some notable people search engines:

- ZoomInfo: Offers real-time data from various sources.

- Pipl Pro: Provides real-time information but requires a subscription.

- Intelius: Searches public records for accurate reports.

- LexisNexis Public Records: Contains over 83 billion public records.

- PeopleSmart: Offers a wide range of information but lacks report downloads.

- Yasni: Searches across various databases and online platforms.

- FreshAddress: Focuses on delivering accurate contact information.

- EmailSherlock: Conducts reverse email searches.

- Spokeo: Helps find social media profiles.

- MyLife: Aggregates public information for profiles.

How to Conduct a Candidate Search Online

Using Specific Keywords

Make your keywords as specific as possible to improve search accuracy.

Simplify Your Search Terms

Eliminate stop words and use the simplest form of keywords, avoiding plurals and verb forms.

Using Quotation Marks

Quotation marks ensure exact word or phrase matches and eliminate stemmed variations.

Removing Unhelpful Words

Use a hyphen or minus sign before a word to exclude it from the search.

Avoid Search Pitfalls

Be cautious of SEO-optimized content and paid advertisements in search results.

Start Broad and Narrow Down

Begin with broad searches and gradually narrow down your results.

Keep Experimenting

Experiment with different search terms and strategies to refine your sourcing process continually.

Analyzing a Job Description

Review the job description thoroughly to identify keywords and skills to target in your search.

Using a Boolean Generator Tool

Tools like SeekOut's Boolean generator can help streamline the creation of Boolean search strings based on job descriptions.

Generic Boolean Strings

Use these generic Boolean string examples to refine searches for profiles, resumes, directories, events, alumni, layoff lists, and active talent.

Mastering online candidate sourcing requires a combination of advanced search techniques, Boolean operators, and familiarity with specialized search engines and people search directories. By continuously refining your sourcing strategies and adapting to different roles, you can efficiently identify and connect with top talent in the competitive job market. Stay proactive, keep experimenting, and watch your sourcing skills flourish.

Chapter 11: Sourcing on Social Media

In the ever-evolving world of talent acquisition, sourcers and recruiters are continually exploring new avenues to discover top-notch candidates. Social media websites have emerged as a goldmine for sourcing and recruiting talent. In this blog post, we'll explore how sourcers can effectively source and recruit on various social media platforms, including Reddit, Facebook, Discord, Twitter, GitHub, and LinkedIn, and provide real-life examples of recruiters successfully doing so.

Reddit: Tapping into Niche Communities

Why Reddit? Reddit boasts a diverse range of subreddits catering to specific interests and industries. Sourcers can target candidates with highly specialized skills and knowledge.

How to Source on Reddit:

1. Identify relevant subreddits.

2. Build your credibility by actively participating in discussions.

3. Craft personalized messages to potential candidates.

4. Engage authentically and respect privacy.

Real-World Example: A tech company found a skilled Python developer on r/forhire, leading to a successful hire who significantly contributed to their projects.

Facebook: Leverage Groups and Networking

Why Facebook? Facebook offers an extensive network of professionals and groups dedicated to various industries and job opportunities.

How to Source on Facebook:

1. Join industry-specific groups and job boards.

2. Actively participate in group discussions.

3. Connect with potential candidates through messenger.

4. Utilize Facebook Jobs for posting openings.

Real-World Example: A marketing agency sourced a talented content writer from a marketing-focused group, resulting in a valuable addition to their team.

Discord: Engaging in Real-Time

Why Discord? Discord's real-time communication makes it suitable for engaging with candidates and assessing their skills.

How to Source on Discord:

1. Join Discord servers related to your industry.

2. Engage with members in text and voice channels.

3. Share job opportunities and connect directly with potential candidates.

Real-World Example: A gaming company found a passionate game developer on a Discord server, leading to a successful hire who contributed to their game's success.

Twitter: Building a Professional Network

Why Twitter? Twitter's open nature allows recruiters to engage with professionals and discover passive candidates.

How to Source on Twitter:

1. Follow professionals in your industry.

2. Share job openings and industry insights.

3. Use relevant hashtags to increase visibility.

4. Directly message potential candidates.

Real-World Example: A tech startup connected with a talented software engineer on Twitter, resulting in a successful hire who played a crucial role in product development.

GitHub: Unearthing Developers' Repositories

Why GitHub? GitHub is a treasure trove of code repositories, making it ideal for sourcing developers.

How to Source on GitHub:

1. Search for repositories related to your technology stack.

2. Examine contributors' profiles for potential candidates.

3. Reach out to developers through their GitHub profiles.

Real-World Example: A software company discovered a skilled web developer through their contributions to open-source projects on GitHub, leading to a valuable hire.

LinkedIn: The Professional Network

Why LinkedIn? LinkedIn is the go-to platform for professional networking and job searching.

How to Source on LinkedIn:

1. Use advanced search filters to narrow down candidates.

2. Send personalized connection requests and messages.

3. Post job openings on your company's LinkedIn page.

4. Engage with industry-related content.

Real-World Example: A finance company identified a qualified financial analyst on LinkedIn, resulting in a successful hire who enhanced their team's capabilities.

Sourcing and recruiting on social media platforms offer a plethora of opportunities to discover top talent. By leveraging the unique features and strengths of each platform, sourcers and recruiters can expand their talent pool and make strategic hires.

Whether you're exploring niche communities on Reddit or building a professional network on LinkedIn, the key is to approach each platform authentically and respectfully, fostering meaningful connections with potential candidates. Happy sourcing!

Below are some SITE search examples:

GitHub:

1. Search for software engineers by location:

   - **site:github.com location:"San Francisco" software engineer**

   - **site:github.com location:"New York" web developer**

2. Find software engineers with specific skills:

- **site:github.com "machine learning" language:python**

- **site:github.com "full-stack developer" language:javascript**

3. Search for software engineers in specific organizations:

   - **site:github.com org:google software engineer**

   - **site:github.com org:microsoft data scientist**

Stack Overflow:

1. Find software engineers with expertise in certain technologies:

   - **site:stackoverflow.com [python] software engineer**

   - **site:stackoverflow.com [java] web developer**

2. Search for software engineers in specific locations:

   - **site:stackoverflow.com location:"San Francisco" software engineer**

   - **site:stackoverflow.com location:"New York" front-end developer**

3. Look for software engineers with specific reputation levels:

  - **site:stackoverflow.com reputation:>10000 software engineer**

  - **site:stackoverflow.com reputation:5000-10000 data scientist**

Twitter:

1. Search for software engineers using relevant hashtags:

  - **site:twitter.com #softwareengineer**

  - **site:twitter.com #webdeveloper**

2. Find software engineers in specific locations:

  - **site:twitter.com near:"Los Angeles" software engineer**

  - **site:twitter.com near:"Chicago" data scientist**

3. Look for software engineers based on their bio information:

  - **site:twitter.com bio:"Python developer"**

  - **site:twitter.com bio:"Full-stack engineer"**

Meetup:

1. Search for software engineering meetups:

    - **site:meetup.com "software development" software engineers**

    - **site:meetup.com "web development" developers**

2. Find meetups in specific locations:

    - **site:meetup.com near:"Austin" software engineers**

    - **site:meetup.com near:"Seattle" front-end developers**

3. Search for meetups organized by specific groups:

    - **site:meetup.com organizer:"Tech Enthusiasts" software engineers**

    - **site:meetup.com organizer:"JavaScript Wizards" web developers**

LinkedIn:

1. Find software engineers by job title:

    - **site:linkedin.com title:"Software Engineer"**

    - **site:linkedin.com title:"Front-end Developer"**

2. Search for software engineers based on skills:

   - **site:linkedin.com skills:"Java" software engineer**

   - **site:linkedin.com skills:"Machine Learning" data scientist**

3. Look for software engineers in specific locations:

   - **site:linkedin.com location:"San Francisco Bay Area" software engineer**

   - **site:linkedin.com location:"New York City" web developer**

Chapter 12: Recruiter Outreach Examples

Recruiting top talent is a challenging task, and one of the most critical steps in the process is reaching out to potential candidates. The way you craft your outreach messages can significantly impact a candidate's perception of your organization and their willingness to engage in the hiring process. In this blog post, we'll explore best practices for recruiter outreach messages and provide examples to help you connect with candidates effectively.

Best Practices for Recruiter Outreach Messages

1. **Personalization is Key:**

   - Address candidates by their name and reference their skills, experience, or achievements. Show that you've done your homework and that your message isn't generic.

2. **Clear and Engaging Subject Lines:**

   - Your subject line should grab the candidate's attention and give them a reason to open the message. Avoid using vague or spammy subject lines.

3. **Concise and Respectful:**

- Keep your message concise and to the point. Candidates appreciate brevity. Respect their time by getting to the main point quickly.

4. **Highlight Value Proposition:**

   - Clearly communicate what makes your organization unique and why the candidate should consider your opportunity. Emphasize how the role aligns with their career goals.

5. **Show Enthusiasm:**

   - Express genuine enthusiasm about the candidate's potential fit for the role and your excitement to speak with them. Authenticity goes a long way.

6. **Provide Contact Information:**

   - Make it easy for candidates to reach out to you. Include your contact information and encourage them to ask questions or seek clarification.

7. **Opt for Mobile-Friendly Formatting:**

   - Many candidates check emails on mobile devices. Ensure your message is easily readable on smartphones and tablets.

8. **A/B Testing:**

- Experiment with different messaging approaches and subject lines to see which ones yield the best response rates. Adjust your strategy accordingly.

Example Recruiter Outreach Messages

Example 1: Reaching Out to a Passive Candidate

Subject Line: Exciting Opportunity for a [Role] at [Company Name]

Hi [Candidate's Name],

I hope this message finds you well. I came across your impressive background in [relevant skill/experience] and couldn't help but reach out. At [Company Name], we're on the lookout for exceptional talent like yourself to join our team.

Our company is known for [mention a unique selling point or achievement], and we believe your expertise would be a valuable addition. I'd love to discuss how your skills align with our open [Role] position.

If you're open to a conversation, please let me know your availability, and we can schedule a brief call at your convenience. I look forward to the possibility of working together.

Best regards, [Your Name] [Your Contact Information]

Example 2: Reaching Out to an Active Job Seeker

Subject Line: Your Dream Role: [Role] at [Company Name]

Hi [Candidate's Name],

I hope you're having a great day. I noticed your interest in [specific skill or industry] roles and wanted to share an exciting opportunity with you.

At [Company Name], we're actively seeking a [Role] who shares our passion for [mention a relevant aspect of the company's mission or values]. Your background in [relevant experience] aligns perfectly with what we're looking for.

I'd love to connect and discuss how this role could be a fantastic fit for your career goals. When you have a moment, let's schedule a time to chat. Feel free to reach out to me at [Your Contact Information].

Looking forward to the possibility of working together! Best regards, [Your Name]

These examples demonstrate the importance of personalization, enthusiasm, and clarity in recruiter outreach messages. By following best practices and crafting thoughtful messages, you can engage candidates more effectively and build positive relationships throughout the hiring process.

If you need more examples, I recommend reading my other book: "The Art of the Recruiter Message."

Chapter 13: Talent Sourcing Jam

One of the most valuable assets in the world of recruitment is a strong network of referrals. Referral candidates tend to be a better fit culturally, onboard faster, and often have longer tenures within an organization.

To harness the power of referrals, it's essential to create a talent sourcing referral drive. In this blog post, we will explore how to collaborate with hiring managers and their teams to launch a successful referral program that attracts top talent.

Step 1: Align with Hiring Managers
The first step in creating a talent sourcing referral drive is to align with hiring managers. Establish clear communication channels and discuss the following aspects:

Understanding the Hiring Needs: Ensure that you have a deep understanding of the roles hiring managers are looking to fill. This knowledge is essential to target your sourcing efforts effectively.
Benefits of Referrals: Explain the benefits of hiring through referrals. Hiring managers should understand that referrals often result in high-quality candidates who are more likely to succeed in the organization.
Expectations: Set clear expectations regarding the volume of referrals needed and the timeline for sourcing. Ensure that both parties are on the same page when it comes to goals and outcomes.

Pro Tip: Ensure that you retrieve your recruiting data and incorporate it into your meeting with the hiring manager. This data can help demonstrate the effectiveness of direct referral programs by showcasing the specific number of hires that have been successfully sourced through these programs.

Step 2: Collaborative Strategy Development
Work collaboratively with hiring managers and their teams to develop a strategy for the referral drive. Consider the following elements:

Target Candidate Personas: Use your talent mapping data to identify ideal candidate personas. Share this information with hiring managers to help them understand the characteristics of the candidates you're seeking.
Sourcing Channels: Discuss the most effective sourcing channels for referrals. Consider internal networks, industry events, alumni associations, and professional organizations.
Employee Engagement: Encourage hiring managers and their teams to actively participate in the referral drive. Their engagement and enthusiasm will inspire others to participate.

Step 3: Training and Education
Organize training sessions or workshops to educate hiring managers and their teams on the art of making quality referrals. Cover the following topics:

Referral Criteria: Clearly define what makes a strong referral. Highlight the skills, experience, and cultural fit factors that should be considered.

Referral Process: Walk through the referral process, from identifying potential candidates to submitting referrals. Ensure that everyone understands the steps involved.

Benefits and Rewards: Explain any incentives or rewards for successful referrals. This can be monetary bonuses, recognition, or other perks.

Step 4: Communication and Promotion

Promote the referral drive within the organization and among hiring managers. Use various communication channels, such as:

Internal Emails: Send out regular updates and reminders about the referral drive through internal email communication.

Intranet and Company Newsletters: Utilize your company's intranet and newsletters to feature success stories and highlight the impact of referrals.

Meetings and Town Halls: Discuss the referral drive during team meetings and company town hall sessions. Encourage hiring managers to share their involvement.

Step 5: Tracking and Reporting

Implement a tracking system to monitor the progress of the referral drive. Keep hiring managers and their teams informed about the results. Consider using metrics such as:

Number of Referrals: Track the total number of referrals received from each team or department.
Quality of Referrals: Evaluate the quality of referrals by assessing how many of them progress through the recruitment process.
Time-to-Hire: Measure how long it takes for referred candidates to be hired compared to candidates from other sources.

Step 6: Recognize and Reward
Recognize and reward the efforts of hiring managers and their teams. Acknowledge their contributions and celebrate the success of the referral drive. Rewards can include:

Bonuses: Provide monetary bonuses for successful referrals, with higher rewards for particularly exceptional referrals.
Recognition: Highlight the top referrers in company-wide communications or during meetings.
Exclusive Events: Offer invitations to exclusive events or experiences as a token of appreciation.

Step 7: Continuous Improvement
Continuously evaluate and refine the referral drive based on feedback and results. Gather input from hiring managers and their teams on what worked well and what could be improved. Use this feedback to enhance the program in the future.

Creating a talent sourcing referral drive with the collaboration of hiring managers and their teams can be a game-changer in your recruitment efforts. By aligning goals, developing a strategy, providing training, promoting the drive, tracking progress, and recognizing contributions, you can build a thriving referral program that consistently brings top talent into your organization. Remember, the key to success lies in the partnership and commitment of everyone involved.

Chapter 14: Creating Talent Sourcing Sprints

Talent acquisition is a race against time, and finding the right candidates quickly can make all the difference in securing top talent for your organization. That's where the concept of a "Talent Sourcing Sprint" comes into play. In this blog post, we'll guide you through the steps to create and execute an effective Talent Sourcing Sprint that will help you identify and engage with top candidates swiftly.

What Is a Talent Sourcing Sprint?
A Talent Sourcing Sprint is a focused and time-bound effort to identify, engage, and connect with potential candidates for specific job openings. It's a structured approach that encourages sourcers and recruiters to work efficiently and collaboratively to meet hiring goals within a defined timeframe. Here's how you can create and execute your own Talent Sourcing Sprint:

Step 1: Define Your Sprint Objective
- Start by setting a clear and specific objective for your Talent Sourcing Sprint. Ask yourself questions like:
- What role are you sourcing for?
- How many qualified candidates do you need to identify?
- What is the timeframe for this sprint? (e.g., one week, two weeks)
- Having a well-defined objective will keep your team focused and motivated throughout the sprint.

Step 2: Assemble Your Sourcing Team
Collaboration is key to a successful Talent Sourcing Sprint. Gather a team of sourcers, recruiters, and any other stakeholders necessary for the specific role you're sourcing for. Ensure that everyone understands their roles and responsibilities.

Step 3: Identify Key Sourcing Channels
Determine which sourcing channels are most likely to yield the best candidates for your open position. This may include:
- LinkedIn
- Job boards
- Social media platforms
- Talent databases
- Industry-specific forums or communities

Each channel may require different search strategies and approaches, so be prepared to tailor your efforts accordingly.

Step 4: Develop a Sourcing Strategy
Create a detailed sourcing strategy that outlines how you will search for candidates on each chosen channel. Consider using Boolean search strings to refine your search and identify candidates with the right skills and qualifications. Document your strategy to ensure consistency and accountability.

Step 5: Set Daily Goals
Break down your sprint objective into daily goals. Determine how many candidates you need to identify, connect with, or screen each day to stay on track.

Setting daily goals will help your team stay focused and measure progress throughout the sprint.

Step 6: Leverage Automation Tools
Sourcing tools and technology can significantly enhance your productivity during a Talent Sourcing Sprint. Utilize applicant tracking systems (ATS), candidate relationship management (CRM) software, and AI-powered sourcing tools to automate repetitive tasks and streamline your workflow.

Step 7: Implement Outreach Strategies
Craft personalized and compelling outreach messages to engage with potential candidates. Whether it's through LinkedIn InMail, email, or other communication channels, make sure your messages are tailored to the candidate's profile and the job opportunity.

Step 8: Monitor Progress
Regularly track and review your progress during the Talent Sourcing Sprint. Are you meeting your daily goals? Are there any challenges or bottlenecks that need to be addressed? Adjust your strategy as needed to optimize results.

Step 9: Collaborate and Communicate
Maintain open communication within your sourcing team. Share insights, best practices, and candidate discoveries. Collaboration can lead to creative solutions and a more efficient sourcing process.

Step 10: Evaluate and Celebrate

At the end of the Talent Sourcing Sprint, evaluate your results against the initial objective. Did you identify the required number of qualified candidates? What worked well, and what could be improved for future sprints? Celebrate your team's efforts and successes.

Creating a Talent Sourcing Sprint can be a game-changer in your talent acquisition efforts.

By setting clear objectives, assembling a dedicated team, and following a well-structured plan, you can quickly identify and engage with top candidates, giving your organization a competitive edge in the hiring process. Remember that continuous improvement is key, so use the insights gained from each sprint to refine your sourcing strategies for even better results in the future.

Chapter 15: Job Fair Events

Job fairs and career networking events provide a fantastic opportunity for job seekers to connect with potential employers and for companies to find top talent. However, organizing and executing such events can be challenging without careful planning. In this blog post, we'll walk you through the essential steps to run an effective job fair or career networking event that benefits both job seekers and employers.

Define Your Event's Purpose and Goals
Before you start planning, it's crucial to have a clear understanding of your event's purpose and goals. Are you aiming to fill specific job positions, build a talent pool, promote your organization's brand, or all of the above? Defining your objectives will help you tailor your event to meet those goals.

Choose the Right Date and Location
Selecting the right date and location is vital for the success of your event. Ensure the date doesn't clash with other major events in your industry or community. The venue should be easily accessible and have enough space to accommodate attendees and exhibitors comfortably. Access to public transportation and ample parking is also a plus.

Pro tip: Consider hosting a virtual job fair. It allows candidates to interact with your company and its culture in a more immersive way.

Secure Exhibitors and Sponsors

Recruiters and employers are key participants in job fairs and networking events. Reach out to them well in advance to secure their participation. Consider offering sponsorship packages that provide branding opportunities and exclusive benefits to incentivize their involvement.

Promote Your Event Effectively
Promotion is key to attracting both job seekers and exhibitors. Utilize various marketing channels, including social media, email marketing, your organization's website, and industry-specific job boards. Craft compelling content that highlights the value of attending your event, such as networking opportunities, workshops, and access to a diverse pool of job candidates.

Plan a Compelling Program
Design an engaging program that appeals to your target audience. Include elements like:

Keynote speakers: Invite industry experts to share valuable insights.
Workshops and seminars: Host sessions on topics like resume building, interview skills, and industry trends.
Networking sessions: Allocate time for attendees to interact with recruiters and exhibitors.
Resume review clinics: Offer attendees the chance to have their resumes critiqued by professionals.
Job posting boards: Display available job openings for job seekers to explore.

Create an Efficient Registration Process

Simplify the registration process for both job seekers and exhibitors. Implement online registration to save time and reduce waiting lines on the day of the event. Ensure that all necessary information is collected during registration, such as contact details and areas of interest.

Provide Supportive Resources
Consider providing resources to help attendees make the most of the event. Create event guides or mobile apps with schedules, maps, and exhibitor information. Offer workshops and coaching sessions to help job seekers enhance their job search skills.

Implement Technology
Leverage technology to streamline event management. Use event management software to track registration, monitor attendance, and gather feedback. Consider setting up a mobile app to provide real-time updates, maps, and a platform for networking among attendees.

Encourage Networking
Facilitate networking opportunities by creating designated areas for interaction. Consider icebreaker activities or speed networking sessions to help attendees connect with potential employers and peers in their field.

Follow Up and Collect Feedback
The event isn't over when attendees leave the venue. Follow up with both job seekers and exhibitors to gather feedback and assess the event's impact. Send thank-you emails, share resources discussed during

the event, and request suggestions for improvement. Use this feedback to make your next event even better.

Running an effective job fair or career networking event requires careful planning, attention to detail, and a commitment to creating value for all participants. By defining your goals, securing exhibitors and sponsors, promoting the event effectively, and providing a well-structured program, you can organize an event that benefits job seekers and employers alike.

Use technology to streamline event management and follow up to gather feedback and continuously improve your future events. With the right approach, your job fair or career networking event can become a valuable resource for both job seekers and the organizations looking to hire them.

Chapter 16: Creating a Personal Brand

In the dynamic world of talent sourcing, building a personal brand is no longer optional—it's essential. A strong online presence can set you apart, attract top candidates, and establish you as a trusted industry expert. In this blog post, we'll explore how sourcers can create a compelling personal brand online and provide real-world examples to illustrate the power of personal branding in sourcing.

Why Personal Branding Matters for Sourcers
Your personal brand is the image and reputation you build online through your professional presence, content, and interactions.

Here's why it's crucial for sourcers:

Attract Top Talent: A strong personal brand can make candidates more willing to engage with you and your organization.

Establish Expertise: It showcases your expertise in sourcing and your industry, instilling confidence in candidates.

Build Trust: An authentic and consistent personal brand fosters trust with potential candidates.

Networking: A robust online presence facilitates networking and collaboration with industry peers.

Now, let's dive into the steps to create your personal brand as a sourcer, supported by real-life examples.

1. Define Your Niche
Successful personal branding starts with defining your niche. What industries, roles, or sectors are you most passionate about and experienced in? Choose an area that genuinely interests you and aligns with your sourcing goals.

Example: Sarah Johnson, a technical sourcer, focuses her personal brand on sourcing software engineers with expertise in artificial intelligence. Her LinkedIn profile showcases her passion for AI and her contributions to AI-focused communities.

2. Optimize Your LinkedIn Profile
LinkedIn is a primary platform for sourcers to connect with candidates. Ensure your LinkedIn profile reflects your personal brand. Key elements include:

Professional Headshot: Use a high-quality, friendly headshot that conveys approachability.

Engaging Headline: Craft a captivating headline that showcases your niche and expertise.

Summary: Write a concise yet compelling summary that highlights your sourcing journey and passion for helping candidates find their dream roles.

Example: John Nguyen, a healthcare sourcer, includes "Passionate Healthcare Talent Sourcer" in his LinkedIn headline and provides a summary describing his dedication to connecting healthcare professionals with meaningful careers.

3. Share Valuable Content
Position yourself as a knowledge source by sharing insightful content related to your niche. Write articles, share industry news, and offer tips that benefit your target candidates.

Example: Emma Patel, a finance sourcer, regularly publishes articles on LinkedIn about financial career trends, interview tips, and industry insights. Her content showcases her expertise and provides value to finance professionals.

4. Engage Authentically
Engagement is key to building relationships with candidates. Respond to comments on your posts, participate in relevant discussions, and connect with potential candidates genuinely.

Example: Michael Carter, an IT sourcer, engages with his connections by actively commenting on their posts, sharing relevant job openings, and offering advice to IT professionals. His interactions showcase his commitment to candidate success.

5. Attend Webinars and Conferences
Participating in webinars and conferences, whether as a speaker or attendee, can elevate your personal brand. Share your takeaways and insights from these events on your social media platforms.

Example: Lisa Martinez, a marketing sourcer, regularly attends marketing conferences and live-tweets key insights from industry experts. Her active participation demonstrates her dedication to staying up-to-date in her field.

6. Build a Portfolio
Create a digital portfolio showcasing your successful sourcing projects. Highlight case studies, before-and-after stories, and testimonials from candidates you've placed.

Example: James Collins, an executive sourcer, maintains a website where he shares detailed success stories of executive placements. His portfolio provides tangible evidence of his sourcing expertise.

7. Seek Recommendations
Request recommendations from candidates you've successfully placed. These endorsements serve as powerful testimonials for your personal brand.

Example: Maria Rodriguez, a hospitality sourcer, has a LinkedIn section dedicated to recommendations from grateful candidates who landed their dream jobs through her assistance. These endorsements build trust with potential candidates.

8. Consistency is Key
Consistency is essential in personal branding. Ensure that your online presence—whether on LinkedIn, Twitter, or other platforms—reflects the same niche, values, and messaging.

Example: Richard Clark, a sourcer in the renewable energy sector, maintains a consistent branding across all platforms. His messaging, visuals, and content reinforce his dedication to sustainability in the energy industry.

Creating a personal brand as a sourcer is a journey that involves defining your niche, optimizing your online presence, sharing valuable content, and engaging authentically with candidates.

By following these steps and drawing inspiration from real-life examples, you can establish a personal brand that not only attracts top talent but also positions you as a trusted sourcing expert in your chosen field. Start crafting your personal brand today, and watch your sourcing efforts flourish.

Chapter 17: Employer Branding

Employer branding is the process of shaping and promoting your organization's reputation as an employer of choice. It encompasses the values, culture, and overall image your company projects to potential employees. A strong employer brand not only attracts top talent but also helps retain and engage current employees.

Why Is Employer Branding Important for Recruiters?
Attracting Top Talent: A well-defined employer brand helps you attract candidates who are a good cultural fit and align with your organization's values.

Reducing Recruitment Costs: When your organization is known for its positive work environment and values, you're more likely to receive applications from candidates who are genuinely interested, reducing the need for extensive candidate sourcing and advertising.

Improving Employee Retention: Employees who join an organization aligned with their values are more likely to stay, reducing turnover and associated recruitment costs.
Enhancing Company Reputation: A strong employer brand not only attracts talent but also enhances your company's overall reputation, which can positively impact your customer and client relationships.

How to Use Employer Branding to Source Talent Online

Develop a Strong Online Presence
Establish and maintain a robust online presence through your company's website, social media platforms, and professional networking sites like LinkedIn. Share content that showcases your organization's culture, values, and achievements. Highlight employee success stories, company events, and community involvement to give potential candidates an inside look at your workplace.

Craft an Authentic Employer Value Proposition (EVP)
Your EVP is the unique set of attributes and benefits that your organization offers to employees. It should reflect your company's culture, values, and the overall employee experience. Communicate your EVP clearly in job listings, career pages, and social media profiles to attract candidates who resonate with it.

Leverage Employee Advocacy
Encourage your current employees to become brand advocates. Their positive experiences and endorsements can be powerful tools for attracting new talent. Create programs that incentivize employees to share job openings, company news, and their own work experiences on social media.

Use Visual Storytelling
Visual content, such as videos, photos, and infographics, can provide a more immersive and engaging experience for potential candidates. Create videos showcasing your workplace, employee

testimonials, and day-in-the-life profiles to give candidates a better sense of what it's like to work at your organization.

Engage with Potential Candidates
Interact with potential candidates on social media and professional networking sites. Respond to comments and messages promptly and professionally. Engaging in meaningful conversations helps build relationships and can lead to valuable connections.

Showcase Employee Development
Highlight opportunities for professional growth and development within your organization. Potential candidates are often attracted to companies that invest in their employees' skill development and career progression.

Monitor Online Reviews and Feedback
Keep an eye on employee reviews on websites like Glassdoor and Indeed. Address concerns and issues raised by current or former employees promptly and professionally. Demonstrating that you value employee feedback can improve your employer brand.

Measure Your Impact
Track the effectiveness of your employer branding efforts. Use analytics to monitor the reach and engagement of your online content. Analyze the source of your job applicants to determine which channels are most effective in sourcing tale

Below are some social media post examples:

Job Opportunity Announcement:
"Exciting job opportunity alert! We're looking for a [Job Title] to join our team. If you're passionate about [relevant industry/field], apply now and be part of our dynamic team. Learn more [link to job posting]. #JobOpening #HiringNow"

Highlight Company Culture:
"At [Company Name], we believe in fostering a culture of innovation and inclusivity. Join us in creating a workplace where your ideas are valued. Explore our career opportunities today! #CompanyCulture #WorkplaceCulture"

Employee Testimonial:
"Meet [Employee Name], our [Job Title]. They love working at [Company Name] because [highlight a positive aspect of the company culture or work environment]. Interested in joining our team? Check out our open positions! #EmployeeTestimonial #WorkLife"

Promote a Virtual Event or Webinar:
"Calling all [Industry/Field] professionals! Don't miss our upcoming webinar on [relevant topic]. Join industry experts and network with peers. Reserve your spot now [link to registration]. #Webinar #Networking"

Share Industry Insights:
"Stay up-to-date with the latest trends in [industry/field]. Our experts have shared some valuable insights in our latest blog post. Read it here

[link to the blog]. #IndustryInsights
#ProfessionalDevelopment"

Celebrate Achievements:
"We're proud to announce that [Company Name] has been recognized as [award/accolade]. Join our award-winning team and be part of our success story. Explore our job openings today! #AwardWinningTeam #SuccessStory"

Diversity and Inclusion Focus:
"Diversity makes us stronger. At [Company Name], we're committed to building a diverse and inclusive workplace. Learn about our initiatives and join us in making a difference. #DiversityandInclusion #EqualOpportunity"

Recruitment Event Announcement:
"Join us at our upcoming virtual recruitment event! Meet our team, learn about our company culture, and explore job opportunities. RSVP now [link to event registration]. #RecruitmentEvent #JobFair"

Highlight Employee Benefits:
"At [Company Name], we care about your well-being. Enjoy benefits like flexible work hours, professional development opportunities, and more. Explore our open positions and join a company that values you. #EmployeeBenefits #WorkLifeBalance"

Interactive Poll or Question:
"What do you value most in a workplace? A) Great company culture B) Competitive salary C) Professional growth opportunities. Comment with

your choice below! #WorkplacePreferences #Engagement"

Thankful Thursday:
"It's #ThankfulThursday, and we want to express our gratitude to our amazing team. Thank you for your hard work and dedication. Interested in becoming part of our incredible workforce? Check out our job openings! #Gratitude #JoinUs"

Employee Spotlight:
"Meet [Employee Name], our [Job Title]. They bring creativity and passion to our team every day. Want to be a part of our innovative group? Explore our current job opportunities! #EmployeeSpotlight #TeamWork"
Remember to include relevant hashtags, compelling visuals, and links to job postings or relevant content when posting on social media. Tailoring your posts to your target audience's interests and needs can significantly enhance your recruitment efforts on social media platforms.

Chapter 18: The Future of Talent Sourcing

Talent sourcing has come a long way from traditional methods of job postings and paper resumes. As technology continues to advance at an unprecedented pace, the landscape of talent acquisition is undergoing a profound transformation. In this blog, we'll explore predictions for the future of talent sourcing and the exciting possibilities it holds.

1. AI and Automation Take Center Stage

Prediction: Artificial Intelligence (AI) and automation will become integral to talent sourcing, automating repetitive tasks, and providing data-driven insights. AI and automation are already making waves in talent acquisition. AI-powered tools can sift through thousands of resumes in seconds, matching candidates with job requirements more efficiently. In the future, we can expect AI to:

Predict Candidate Success: AI algorithms will analyze historical hiring data to predict which candidates are most likely to succeed in specific roles.

Chatbots for Candidate Interaction: Chatbots will handle initial candidate interactions, scheduling interviews, and answering FAQs, freeing up recruiters for higher-level tasks.

Automated Candidate Engagement: AI will personalize and automate candidate engagement, nurturing relationships with potential hires over time.

2. Data-Driven Decision Making

Prediction: Recruiters will increasingly rely on data analytics to inform their sourcing strategies, leading to more successful hires.

Data analytics tools are evolving to provide actionable insights into the entire recruitment process. Predictive analytics will:

Identify Sourcing Channels: Recruiters will use data to determine which sourcing channels deliver the highest-quality candidates.

Reduce Bias: Data-driven hiring decisions will help mitigate bias, leading to more diverse and inclusive workplaces.

Improve Candidate Experience: Analytics will pinpoint areas where the candidate experience can be enhanced, reducing drop-offs during the application process.

3. Enhanced Candidate Experience

Prediction: Candidate experience will be a top priority, with personalized and streamlined processes becoming the norm.

The future of talent sourcing will prioritize the candidate journey. Expect to see:

Personalization: Sourcing strategies will be tailored to individual candidates, offering job recommendations and content that match their interests.

Seamless Mobile Experience: Mobile-optimized applications and communication channels will be standard to accommodate candidates on the go.

AI-Powered Feedback: Candidates will receive personalized feedback, even if they don't advance in the hiring process, improving their perception of your company.

4. Social Media and Online Communities
Prediction: Recruiters will tap into online communities and social media platforms to source candidates and build talent pipelines.
As online communities continue to grow, recruiters will:

Engage with Niche Communities: Recruiters will actively participate in online forums, groups, and communities related to their industries to identify top talent.
Leverage Social Media: Platforms like LinkedIn, Twitter, and even emerging platforms will play a crucial role in talent sourcing.
Build Talent Pipelines: Recruiters will nurture relationships within these communities, creating a pool of engaged, pre-qualified candidates.

5. Skills-Based Hiring
Prediction: The emphasis will shift from degrees and certifications to specific skills and capabilities.
In the future, employers will focus on:

Skills Assessments: Skills assessments and practical tests will be common in the hiring process, allowing candidates to showcase their abilities.
Continuous Learning: Hiring based on skills encourages continuous learning, fostering a culture of growth within organizations.

Upskilling and Reskilling: Employers will invest in upskilling and reskilling programs to bridge skill gaps in their workforce.

6. Remote and Hybrid Workforces

Prediction: Remote and hybrid work arrangements will continue to rise, expanding the talent pool for companies. The acceptance of remote work will:

Broaden Geographic Reach: Companies will hire talent from anywhere in the world, increasing diversity.

Flexible Work Models: Hybrid models will offer flexibility, allowing employees to choose when and where they work.

New Sourcing Strategies: Recruiters will adapt their strategies to target remote and globally dispersed candidates.

7. Ethical AI and Data Privacy

Prediction: Ethical considerations around AI and data privacy will shape talent sourcing practices. Recruiters will:

Ensure Fairness: AI algorithms will be carefully monitored and adjusted to prevent bias and discrimination.

Transparent Data Usage: Candidates will have more visibility into how their data is used in the hiring process.

Compliance with Regulations: Companies will invest in compliance with evolving data protection regulations.

8. Gig Economy Integration

Prediction: Traditional employment models will coexist with the gig economy, and recruiters will adapt to source both full-time and freelance talent. Recruiters will:

Source Freelancers: Gig workers will be a valuable resource for short-term projects, and recruiters will incorporate them into their talent pipelines.

Match Skillsets: Recruiters will identify candidates with specialized skills for gig opportunities, leading to more efficient project staffing.

Conclusion:

I trust that you have acquired valuable insights into the realm of talent sourcing through the content of these chapters. Writing on various topics within recruiting has been a rewarding journey, and the heartfelt notes and messages I've received from recruiters worldwide have been deeply appreciated. I cannot express my gratitude enough for the enlightenment and humility this experience has brought me.

I would greatly appreciate it if you could spare a moment to share your honest review of this book. Your feedback will help others benefit from this series as well.

Please follow WizardSourcer.com for my latest updates.